The Greatest Quotes From The Greatest People

Inspire and motivate yourself
The best book for success,
happiness and improvement

George P.

GEORGE P.

Copyright © 2017 George P.

All rights reserved.

ISBN: 978-1-9734-1452-0

CONTENTS

	Introduction	i
1	Business	1
2	Life	9
3	Motivation	17
4	Politics	26
5	Success	34
6	Authors' Biographies	48

INTRODUCTION

Life is an unexpected journey. No matter how prepared, strong or educated you are, there are always times when everything falls apart. This book aims to keep you passionate about your daily life and motivate you during difficult periods. These 491 quotes from 309 authors are a must-have gift for yourself or your loved ones.
The most successful people since 600 BC teach us how to thrive in both personal and professional life. This book includes the best quotes of five categories: business, life, motivation, politics and success. The aforementioned chapters include everything people should always bear in mind, despite their age or occupation. Either you are a professor or an athlete, a millionaire or bankrupt, student or elderly, have many friends or enemies, this is the best book to change your perspectives on life.
The Greatest Quotes From The Greatest People is an essential book for those who want to develop themselves, be happy, and appreciate life.
The authors of these quotes have diverse backgrounds; billionaires, philosophers, scientists, managers, teachers, generals, presidents, artists and many more share their wisdom.
In the last chapter, you can discover details such as date of birth, occupation and a brief biography of every author mentioned in this book.

For my love, Ioanna
George
The United Kingdom, 2017

1 BUSINESS

Great things in business are never done by one person. They're done by a team of people.
Steve Jobs (1955-2011)

If people like you, they'll listen to you, but if they trust you, they'll do business with you.
Zig Ziglar (1926-2012)

I never called my work an 'art'. It's part of show business, the business of building entertainment.
Walt Disney (1901-1966)

Whenever you find yourself on the side of the majority, it is time to pause and reflect.
Mark Twain (1835-1910)

A passionate belief in your business and personal objectives can make all the difference between success and failure. If you aren't proud of what you're doing, why should anybody else be?
Richard Branson (1950-)

A satisfied customer is the best business strategy of all.
Michael LeBoeuf (1942-)

The business of art is to reveal the relation between man and his environment.
D. H. Lawrence (1885-1930)

We're all working together; that's the secret.
Sam Walton (1918-1992)

A brand for a company is like a reputation for a person. You earn reputation by trying to do hard things well.
Jeff Bezos (1964-)

The first rule of any technology used in a business is that automation applied to an efficient operation will magnify the efficiency. The second is that automation applied to an inefficient operation will magnify the inefficiency.

Bill Gates (1955-)

Information technology and business are becoming inextricably interwoven. I don't think anybody can talk meaningfully about one without the talking about the other.
Bill Gates (1955-)

Ideas pull the trigger, but instinct loads the gun.
Don Marquis (1878-1937)

A business that makes nothing but money is a poor business.
Henry Ford (1863-1947)

Details create the big picture.
Sanford I. Weill (1933-)

Good business leaders create a vision, articulate the vision, passionately own the vision and relentlessly drive it to completion.
Jack Welch (1935-)

Brand is just a perception and perception will match reality over time. Sometimes it will be ahead, other times it will be behind. But brand is simply a collective impression some have about a product.
Elon Musk (1971-)

There is only one boss. The customer. And he can fire everybody in the company from the chairman on down, simply by spending his money somewhere else.
Sam Walton (1918-1992)

In the business world, the rearview mirror is always clearer than the windshield.
Warren Buffett (1930-)

Before you can become a millionaire, you must learn to think like one. You must learn how to motivate yourself to counter fear with courage. Making critical decisions about your career, business, investments and other resources conjures up fear, fear that is part of the process of becoming a financial success.
Thomas J. Stanley (1944-2015)

If one does not know to which port one is sailing, no wind is favorable.

THE GREATEST QUOTES FROM THE GREATEST PEOPLE

Lucius Annaeus Seneca (4 BC-65)

The entrepreneur always searches for change, responds to it and exploits it as an opportunity.
Peter Drucker (1909-2005)

Business has only two functions - marketing and innovation.
Milan Kundera (1929-)

Sales are contingent upon the attitude of the salesman - not the attitude of the prospect.
W. Clement Stone (1902-2002)

The superior man understands what is right; the inferior man understands what will sell.
Confucius (551 BC-479 BC)

An organization's ability to learn and translate that learning into action rapidly, is the ultimate competitive advantage.
Jack Welch (1935-)

A friendship founded on business is better than a business founded on friendship.
John D. Rockefeller (1839-1937)

If you're trying to create a company, it's like baking a cake. You have to have all the ingredients in the right proportion.
Elon Musk (1971-)

Don't ever let your business get ahead of the financial side of your business. Accounting, accounting, accounting. Know your numbers.
Tilman J. Fertitta (1957-)

The first responsibility of a leader is to define reality. The last is to say thank you. In between, the leader is a servant.
Max de Pree (1924-2017)

From my very first day as an entrepreneur, I've felt the only mission worth pursuing in business is to make people's lives better.
Richard Branson (1950-)

What helps people, helps business.

GEORGE P.

Leo Burnett (1891-1971)

Rank does not confer privilege or give power. It imposes responsibility.
Peter Drucker (1909-2005)

Business is about people. It's about passion. It's about bold ideas, bold small ideas or bold large ideas.
Tom Peters (1942-)

Business opportunities are like buses, there's always another one coming.
Richard Branson (1950-)

We need business to understand its social responsibility, that the main task and objective for a business is not to generate extra income and to become rich and transfer the money abroad, but to look and evaluate what a businessman has done for the country, for the people, on whose account he or she has become so rich.
Vladimir Putin (1952-)

I think a simple rule of business is, if you do the things that are easier first, then you can actually make a lot of progress.
Mark Zuckerberg (1984-)

The golden rule for every businessman is this: 'Put yourself in your customer's place.'
Orison Swett Marden (1848-1924)

We're in the business of selling pleasure. We don't sell handbags or haute couture. We sell dreams.
Alain Wertheimer (1948-)

I think that in any group activity - whether it be business, sports, or family - there has to be leadership or it won't be successful.
John Wooden (1910-2010)

Just because something doesn't do what you planned it to do doesn't mean it's useless.
Thomas A. Edison (1847-1931)

Time is the scarcest resource and unless it is managed nothing else can be managed.
Peter Drucker (1909-2005)

People are definitely a company's greatest asset. It doesn't make any difference whether the product is cars or cosmetics. A company is only as good as the people it keeps.
Mary Kay Ash (1918-2001)

Great companies are built on great products.
Elon Musk (1971-)

Information technology is at the core of how you do your business and how your business model itself evolves.
Satya Nadella (1967-)

Product management really is the fusion between technology, what engineers do - and the business side.
Marissa Mayer (1975-)

Everyone has an invisible sign hanging from their neck saying, 'Make me feel important.' Never forget this message when working with people.
Mary Kay Ash (1918-2001)

The true measure of the value of any business leader and manager is performance.
Brian Tracy (1944-)

In almost every profession - whether it's law or journalism, finance or medicine or academia or running a small business - people rely on confidential communications to do their jobs. We count on the space of trust that confidentiality provides. When someone breaches that trust, we are all worse off for it.
Hillary Clinton (1947-)

The business of business is relationships; the business of life is human connection.
Robin S. Sharma (1965-)

My model for business is The Beatles: They were four guys that kept each other's negative tendencies in check; they balanced each other. And the total was greater than the sum of the parts.
Steve Jobs (1955-2011)

Investing in management means building communication systems, business

processes, feedback and routines that let you scale the business and team as efficiently as possible.
Fred Wilson (1961-)

Some people regard private enterprise as a predatory tiger to be shot. Others look on it as a cow they can milk. Not enough people see it as a healthy horse, pulling a sturdy wagon.
Winston Churchill (1874-1965)

It is rare to find a business partner who is selfless. If you are lucky it happens once in a lifetime.
Michael Eisner (1942-)

Sweat equity is the most valuable equity there is. Know your business and industry better than anyone else in the world. Love what you do or don't do it.
Mark Cuban (1958-)

Most of what we call management consists of making it difficult for people to get their work done.
Peter Drucker (1909-2005)

Competition is the keen cutting edge of business, always shaving away at costs.
Henry Ford (1863-1947)

There is an immutable conflict at work in life and in business, a constant battle between peace and chaos. Neither can be mastered, but both can be influenced. How you go about that is the key to success.
Phil Knight (1938-)

Our work is the presentation of our capabilities.
Edward Gibbon (1737-1794)

As you grow in this business, you learn how to do more with less.
Morgan Freeman (1937-)

If you don't understand the details of your business, you are going to fail.
Jeff Bezos (1964-)

You're either making money or you're not. If you're not making money get out of the business.

THE GREATEST QUOTES FROM THE GREATEST PEOPLE

Meredith Whitney (1969-)

Sometimes when you innovate, you make mistakes. It is best to admit them quickly and get on with improving your other innovations.
Steve Jobs (1955-2011)

Employers have recognized for some time that it's smart business to have a diverse workforce - one in which many views are represented and everyone's talents are valued. Well, disability is part of diversity.
Thomas Perez (1961-)

People are in such a hurry to launch their product or business that they seldom look at marketing from a bird's eye view and they don't create a systematic plan.
Dave Ramsey (1960-)

Few businessmen are capable of being in politics, they don't understand the democratic process, they have neither the tolerance nor the depth it takes. Democracy isn't a business.
Malcolm Forbes (1919-1990)

I'm not a driven businessman, but a driven artist. I never think about money. Beautiful things make money.
Lord Acton (1834-1902)

I believe you have to be willing to be misunderstood if you're going to innovate.
Jeff Bezos (1964-)

Business is a team sport.
Greg Brenneman (1961-)

Profitability is coming from productivity, efficiency, management, austerity and the way to manage the business.
Carlos Slim (1940-)

To me, job titles don't matter. Everyone is in sales. It's the only way we stay in business.
Harvey Mackay (1932-)

The common question that gets asked in business is, 'why?' That's a good question, but an equally valid question is, 'why not?'

Jeff Bezos (1964-)

The problem is that at a lot of big companies, process becomes a substitute for thinking. You're encouraged to behave like a little gear in a complex machine. Frankly, it allows you to keep people who aren't that smart, who aren't that creative.
Elon Musk (1971-)

This is a learning in the business life that first of all you need to have commitment, dedication and passion for what you are doing.
Lakshmi Mittal (1950-)

There are two ways to extend a business. Take inventory of what you're good at and extend out from your skills. Or determine what your customers need and work backward, even if it requires learning new skills. Kindle is an example of working backward.
Jeff Bezos (1964-)

If you or I fail at business, we fail. If we cheat and fail, we go to jail. But if you're rich and politically connected, your incompetence may be protected by a government bailout.
Robert Kiyosaki (1947-)

Punctuality is the soul of business.
Thomas Chandler Haliburton (1796-1865)

Personal relationships are always the key to good business. You can buy networking; you can't buy friendships.
Lindsay Fox (1937-)

2 LIFE

Life is 10% what happens to you and 90% how you react to it.
Charles R. Swindoll (1934-)

I love those who can smile in trouble, who can gather strength from distress and grow brave by reflection. 'Tis the business of little minds to shrink, but they whose heart is firm and whose conscience approves their conduct, will pursue their principles unto death.
Leonardo da Vinci (1452-1519)

Only I can change my life. No one can do it for me.
Carol Burnett (1933-)

There is only one happiness in this life, to love and be loved.
George Sand (1804-1876)

Learn to enjoy every minute of your life. Be happy now. Don't wait for something outside of yourself to make you happy in the future. Think how really precious the time is you have to spend, whether it's at work or with your family. Every minute should be enjoyed and savored.
Earl Nightingale (1921-1989)

We must let go of the life we have planned, so as to accept the one that is waiting for us.
Joseph Campbell (1904-1987)

Smile in the mirror. Do that every morning and you'll start to see a big difference in your life.
Yoko Ono (1933-)

My mission in life is not merely to survive, but to thrive; and to do so with some passion, some compassion, some humor and some style.
Maya Angelou (1928-2014)

Life isn't about finding yourself. Life is about creating yourself.
George Bernard Shaw (1856-1950)

It's all about quality of life and finding a happy balance between work and friends and family.
Philip Green (1952-)

GEORGE P.

Death is not the greatest loss in life. The greatest loss is what dies inside us while we live.
Norman Cousins (1915-1990)

Your work is going to fill a large part of your life and the only way to be truly satisfied is to do what you believe is great work. And the only way to do great work is to love what you do. If you haven't found it yet, keep looking. Don't settle. As with all matters of the heart, you'll know when you find it.
Steve Jobs (1955-2011)

Be happy for this moment. This moment is your life.
Omar Khayyam (1048-1131)

There are two great days in a person's life - the day we are born and the day we discover why.
William Barclay (1907-1978)

Because of your smile, you make life more beautiful.
Thich Nhat Hanh (1926-)

It is not length of life, but depth of life.
Ralph Waldo Emerson (1803-1882)

Clouds come floating into my life, no longer to carry rain or usher storm, but to add color to my sunset sky.
Rabindranath Tagore (1861-1941)

Do not take life too seriously. You will never get out of it alive.
Elbert Hubbard (1856-1915)

Do not dwell in the past, do not dream of the future, concentrate the mind on the present moment.
Buddha (563 BC-483 BC)

The good life is one inspired by love and guided by knowledge.
Bertrand Russell (1872-1970)

The biggest adventure you can take is to live the life of your dreams.
Oprah Winfrey (1954-)

THE GREATEST QUOTES FROM THE GREATEST PEOPLE

I have seen many storms in my life. Most storms have caught me by surprise, so I had to learn very quickly to look further and understand that I am not capable of controlling the weather, to exercise the art of patience and to respect the fury of nature.
Paulo Coelho (1947-)

Keep love in your heart. A life without it is like a sunless garden when the flowers are dead.
Oscar Wilde (1854-1900)

If you love life, don't waste time, for time is what life is made up of.
Bruce Lee (1940-1973)

My life motto is 'Do my best, so that I can't blame myself for anything.'
Magdalena Neuner (1987-)

Lighten up, just enjoy life, smile more, laugh more and don't get so worked up about things.
Kenneth Branagh (1960-)

God gave us the gift of life; it is up to us to give ourselves the gift of living well.
Voltaire (1694-1778)

Very little is needed to make a happy life; it is all within yourself, in your way of thinking.
Marcus Aurelius (121-180)

When you rise in the morning, give thanks for the light, for your life, for your strength. Give thanks for your food and for the joy of living. If you see no reason to give thanks, the fault lies in yourself.
Tecumseh (1768-1813)

My greatest beauty secret is being happy with myself. I don't use special creams or treatments - I'll use a little bit of everything. It's a mistake to think you are what you put on yourself. I believe that a lot of how you look is to do with how you feel about yourself and your life. Happiness is the greatest beauty secret.
Tina Turner (1939-)

Your time is limited, so don't waste it living someone else's life. Don't be trapped by dogma - which is living with the results of another people's

thinking. Don't let the noise of others' opinions drown out your own inner voice. And most important, have the courage to follow your heart and intuition.
Steve Jobs (1955-2011)

Life is really simple, but we insist on making it complicated.
Confucius (551 BC-479 BC)

The purpose of art is washing the dust of daily life off our souls.
Pablo Picasso (1881-1973)

Did I offer peace today? Did I bring a smile to someone's face? Did I say words of healing? Did I let go of my anger and resentment? Did I forgive? Did I love? These are the real questions. I must trust that the little bit of love that I sow now will bear many fruits, here in this world and the life to come.
Henri Nouwen (1932-1996)

The unexamined life is not worth living.
Socrates (470 BC-399 BC)

Education is not preparation for life; education is life itself.
John Dewey (1859-1952)

Choose a job you love and you will never have to work a day in your life.
Confucius (551 BC-479 BC)

Life is one big road with lots of signs. So, when you ride through the ruts, don't complicate your mind. Flee from hate, mischief and jealousy. Don't bury your thoughts, put your vision to reality. Wake Up and Live!
Bob Marley (1945-1981)

The more you praise and celebrate your life, the more there is in life to celebrate.
Oprah Winfrey (1954-)

Successful people maintain a positive focus in life no matter what is going on around them. They stay focused on their past successes rather than their past failures and on the next action steps they need to take to get them closer to the fulfillment of their goals rather than all the other distractions that life presents to them.
Jack Canfield (1944-)

Just as a candle cannot burn without fire, men cannot live without a spiritual life.
Buddha (563 BC-483 BC)

Loneliness adds beauty to life. It puts a special burn on sunsets and makes night air smell better.
Henry Rollins (1961-)

Let your life lightly dance on the edges of Time like dew on the tip of a leaf.
Rabindranath Tagore (1861-1941)

The art of living is more like wrestling than dancing.
Marcus Aurelius (121-180)

The more sand that has escaped from the hourglass of our life, the clearer we should see through it.
Jean Paul (1763-1825)

Bad things do happen; how I respond to them defines my character and the quality of my life. I can choose to sit in perpetual sadness, immobilized by the gravity of my loss, or I can choose to rise from the pain and treasure the most precious gift I have - life itself.
Walter Anderson (1903-1965)

The purpose of human life is to serve and to show compassion and the will to help others.
Albert Schweitzer (1875-1965)

Change is the law of life. And those who look only to the past or present are certain to miss the future.
John F. Kennedy (1917-1963)

Instead of trying to make your life perfect, give yourself the freedom to make it an adventure and go ever upward.
Drew Houston (1983-)

Life is like riding a bicycle. To keep your balance, you must keep moving.
Albert Einstein (1879-1955)

Slow down and enjoy life. It's not only the scenery you miss by going too fast - you also miss the sense of where you are going and why.

GEORGE P.

Eddie Cantor (1892-1964)

Life is a dream for the wise, a game for the fool, a comedy for the rich, a tragedy for the poor.
Sholem Aleichem (1859-1916)

Imagination and fiction make up more than three quarters of our real life.
Simone Weil (1909-1943)

With the past, I have nothing to do; nor with the future. I live now.
Ralph Waldo Emerson (1803-1882)

Gratitude unlocks the fullness of life. It turns what we have into enough and more. It turns denial into acceptance, chaos to order, confusion to clarity. It can turn a meal into a feast, a house into a home, a stranger into a friend.
Melody Beattie (1948-)

For life and death are one, even as the river and the sea are one.
Khalil Gibran (1883-1931)

Life is a journey that must be traveled no matter how bad the roads and accommodations.
Oliver Goldsmith (1728-1774)

My theory on life is that life is beautiful. Life doesn't change. You have a day and a night and a month and a year. We people change - we can be miserable or we can be happy. It's what you make of your life.
Mohammed bin Rashid Al Maktoum (1949-)

Life was always a matter of waiting for the right moment to act.
Paulo Coelho (1947-)

Life is a series of natural and spontaneous changes. Don't resist them - that only creates sorrow. Let reality be reality. Let things flow naturally forward in whatever way they like.
Lao Tzu (604 BC-531 BC)

Beginning today, treat everyone you meet as if they were going to be dead by midnight. Extend to them all the care, kindness and understanding you can muster and do it with no thought of any reward. Your life will never be the same again.

THE GREATEST QUOTES FROM THE GREATEST PEOPLE

Og Mandino (1923-1996)

In everyone's life, at some time, our inner fire goes out. It is then burst into flame by an encounter with another human being. We should all be thankful for those people who rekindle the inner spirit.
Albert Schweitzer (1875-1965)

Make it a habit to tell people thank you. To express your appreciation, sincerely and without the expectation of anything in return. Truly appreciate those around you and you'll soon find many others around you. Truly appreciate life and you'll find that you have more of it.
Ralph Marston (1907-1967)

The fear of death follows from the fear of life. A man who lives fully is prepared to die at any time.
Mark Twain (1835-1910)

We do not remember days, we remember moments.
Cesare Pavese (1908-1950)

No matter what has happened to you in the past or what is going on in your life right now, it has no power to keep you from having an amazingly good future if you will walk by faith in God. God loves you! He wants you to live with victory over sin so you can possess His promises for your life today!
Joyce Meyer (1943-)

If you always put limit on everything you do, physical or anything else. It will spread into your work and into your life. There are no limits. There are only plateaus and you must not stay there; you must go beyond them.
Bruce Lee (1940-1973)

You can't connect the dots looking forward; you can only connect them looking backwards. So, you have to trust that the dots will somehow connect in your future. You have to trust in something - your gut, destiny, life, karma, whatever. This approach has never let me down and it has made all the difference in my life.
Steve Jobs (1955-2011)

A hero is someone who has given his or her life to something bigger than oneself.
Joseph Campbell (1904-1987)

GEORGE P.

The most important thing is to enjoy your life - to be happy - it's all that matters.
Audrey Hepburn (1929-1993)

I used to think that the worst thing in life was to end up alone. It's not. The worst thing in life is to end up with people who make you feel alone.
Robin Williams (1951-2014)

Remember your dreams and fight for them. You must know what you want from life. There is just one thing that makes your dream become impossible: the fear of failure.
Paulo Coelho (1947-)

You have enemies? Good. That means you've stood up for something, sometime in your life.
Winston Churchill (1874-1965)

Life is a song - sing it. Life is a game - play it. Life is a challenge - meet it. Life is a dream - realize it. Life is a sacrifice - offer it. Life is love - enjoy it.
Sai Baba (1835-1918)

Without music, life would be a mistake.
Friedrich Nietzsche (1844-1900)

3 MOTIVATION

Optimism is the faith that leads to achievement. Nothing can be done without hope and confidence.
Helen Keller (1880-1968)

Good, better, best. Never let it rest. 'Til your good is better and your better is best.
St. Jerome (347-420)

Effort only fully releases its reward after a person refuses to quit.
Napoleon Hill (1883-1970)

I hated every minute of training, but I said, 'Don't quit. Suffer now and live the rest of your life as a champion.'
Muhammad Ali (1942-2016)

Infuse your life with action. Don't wait for it to happen. Make it happen. Make your own future. Make your own hope. Make your own love. And whatever your beliefs, honor your creator, not by passively waiting for grace to come down from upon high, but by doing what you can to make grace happen... yourself, right now, right down here on Earth.
Bradley Whitford (1959-)

When one must, one can.
Charlotte Whitton (1896-1975)

A somebody was once a nobody who wanted to and did.
John Burroughs (1837-1921)

Failure will never overtake me if my determination to succeed is strong enough.
Og Mandino (1923-1996)

You will never win if you never begin.
Helen Rowland (1875-1950)

It always seems impossible until it's done.
Nelson Mandela (1918-2013)

With the new day comes new strength and new thoughts.

GEORGE P.

Eleanor Roosevelt (1884-1962)

Always do your best. What you plant now, you will harvest later.
Og Mandino (1923-1996)

You have to make it happen.
Denis Diderot (1713-1784)

You can't cross the sea merely by standing and staring at the water.
Rabindranath Tagore (1861-1941)

Quality is not an act; it is a habit.
Aristotle (384 BC-322 BC)

Setting goals is the first step in turning the invisible into the visible.
Tony Robbins (1960-)

Ever tried. Ever failed. No matter. Try Again. Fail again. Fail better.
Samuel Beckett (1906-1989)

Keep your eyes on the stars and your feet on the ground.
Theodore Roosevelt (1858-1919)

The secret of getting ahead is getting started.
Mark Twain (1835-1910)

Our greatest weakness lies in giving up. The most certain way to succeed is always to try just one more time.
Thomas A. Edison (1847-1931)

Believe in yourself! Have faith in your abilities! Without a humble but reasonable confidence in your own powers you cannot be successful or happy.
Norman Vincent Peale (1898-1993)

Your talent is God's gift to you. What you do with it is your gift back to God.
Leo Buscaglia (1924-1998)

The will to win, the desire to succeed, the urge to reach your full potential... these are the keys that will unlock the door to personal excellence.
Confucius (551 BC-479 BC)

THE GREATEST QUOTES FROM THE GREATEST PEOPLE

There is only one corner of the universe you can be certain of improving and that's your own self.
Aldous Huxley (1894-1963)

Do the difficult things while they are easy and do the great things while they are small. A journey of a thousand miles must begin with a single step.
Lao Tzu (604 BC-531 BC)

Accept the challenges so that you can feel the exhilaration of victory.
George S. Patton (1885-1945)

If you fell down yesterday, stand up today.
H. G. Wells (1866-1946)

If you can dream it, you can do it.
Walt Disney (1901-1966)

A creative man is motivated by the desire to achieve, not by the desire to beat others.
Ayn Rand (1905-1982)

You are never too old to set another goal or to dream a new dream.
Les Brown (1945-)

If you want to conquer fear, don't sit home and think about it. Go out and get busy.
Dale Carnegie (1888-1955)

Never, never, never give up.
Winston Churchill (1874-1965)

When something is important enough, you do it even if the odds are not in your favor.
Elon Musk (1971-)

Well done is better than well said.
Benjamin Franklin (1706-1790)

Problems are not stop signs, they are guidelines.
Robert H. Schuller (1926-2015)

GEORGE P.

Do not wait; the time will never be 'just right.' Start where you stand and work with whatever tools you may have at your command and better tools will be found as you go along.
George Herbert (1593-1633)

Consult not your fears but your hopes and your dreams. Think not about your frustrations, but about your unfulfilled potential. Concern yourself not with what you tried and failed in, but with what it is still possible for you to do.
Pope John XXIII (1881-1963)

Be kind whenever possible. It is always possible.
Dalai Lama (1935-)

If you're going through hell, keep going.
Winston Churchill (1874-1965)

Aim for the moon. If you miss, you may hit a star.
W. Clement Stone (1902-2002)

Start where you are. Use what you have. Do what you can.
Arthur Ashe (1943-1993)

We may encounter many defeats, but we must not be defeated.
Maya Angelou (1928-2014)

Perseverance is not a long race; it is many short races one after the other.
Walter Elliot (1888-1958)

Without hard work, nothing grows but weeds.
Gordon B. Hinckley (1910-2008)

Either you run the day or the day runs you.
Jim Rohn (1930-2009)

What you get by achieving your goals is not as important as what you become by achieving your goals.
Zig Ziglar (1926-2012)

Don't watch the clock; do what it does. Keep going.
Sam Levenson (1911-1980)

THE GREATEST QUOTES FROM THE GREATEST PEOPLE

In order to succeed, we must first believe that we can.
Nikos Kazantzakis (1883-1957)

The key is to keep company only with people who uplift you, whose presence calls forth your best.
Epictetus (55-135)

Do you want to know who you are? Don't ask. Act! Action will delineate and define you.
Thomas Jefferson (1743-1826)

Be miserable. Or motivate yourself. Whatever has to be done, it's always your choice.
Wayne Dyer (1940-2015)

What you do today can improve all your tomorrows.
Ralph Marston (1907-1967)

Expect problems and eat them for breakfast.
Alfred A. Montapert (1906-1997)

Never give up, for that is just the place and time that the tide will turn.
Harriet Beecher Stowe (1811-1896)

Things do not happen. Things are made to happen.
John F. Kennedy (1917-1963)

You can never quit. Winners never quit and quitters never win.
Ted Turner (1938-)

A goal is a dream with a deadline.
Napoleon Hill (1883-1970)

Knowing is not enough; we must apply. Willing is not enough; we must do.
Johann Wolfgang von Goethe (1749-1832)

Look up at the stars and not down at your feet. Try to make sense of what you see and wonder about what makes the universe exist. Be curious.
Stephen Hawking (1942-)

Motivation is the art of getting people to do what you want them to do because they want to do it.

GEORGE P.

Dwight D. Eisenhower (1890-1969)

You are not here merely to make a living. You are here in order to enable the world to live more amply, with greater vision, with a finer spirit of hope and achievement. You are here to enrich the world and you impoverish yourself if you forget the errand.
Woodrow Wilson (1856-1924)

The people who influence you are the people who believe in you.
Henry Drummond (1851-1897)

The way to get started is to quit talking and begin doing.
Walt Disney (1901-1966)

Even if you fall on your face, you're still moving forward.
Victor Kiam (1926-2001)

There is no passion to be found playing small - in settling for a life that is less than the one you are capable of living.
Nelson Mandela (1918-2013)

I know where I'm going and I know the truth and I don't have to be what you want me to be. I'm free to be what I want.
Muhammad Ali (1942-2016)

Do something wonderful, people may imitate it.
Albert Schweitzer (1875-1965)

The most effective way to do it, is to do it.
Amelia Earhart (1897-1939)

The more man meditates upon good thoughts, the better will be his world and the world at large.
Confucius (551 BC-479 BC)

Do your work with your whole heart and you will succeed - there's so little competition.
Elbert Hubbard (1856-1915)

No bird soars too high if he soars with his own wings.
William Blake (1757-1827)

THE GREATEST QUOTES FROM THE GREATEST PEOPLE

The ultimate aim of the ego is not to see something, but to be something.
Muhammad Iqbal (1877-1938)

Arriving at one goal is the starting point to another.
John Dewey (1859-1952)

A good plan violently executed now is better than a perfect plan executed next week.
George S. Patton (1885-1945)

The first question which the priest and the Levite asked was: 'If I stop to help this man, what will happen to me?' But... the good Samaritan reversed the question: 'If I do not stop to help this man, what will happen to him?'
Martin Luther King, Jr. (1929-1968)

I learned that we can do anything, but we can't do everything... at least not at the same time. So think of your priorities not in terms of what activities you do, but when you do them. Timing is everything.
Dan Millman (1946-)

Change your life today. Don't gamble on the future, act now, without delay.
Simone de Beauvoir (1908-1986)

Act as if what you do makes a difference. It does.
William James (1842-1910)

If you think you can do it, you can.
John Burroughs (1837-1921)

Every exit is an entry somewhere else.
Tom Stoppard (1937-)

There's a way to do it better - find it.
Thomas A. Edison (1847-1931)

I attribute my success to this - I never gave or took any excuse.
Florence Nightingale (1820-1910)

We aim above the mark to hit the mark.
Ralph Waldo Emerson (1803-1882)

Never give in and never give up.

GEORGE P.

Hubert H. Humphrey (1911-1978)

The harder the conflict, the more glorious the triumph.
Thomas Paine (1737-1809)

Follow your inner moonlight; don't hide the madness.
Allen Ginsberg (1926-1997)

One way to keep momentum going is to have constantly greater goals.
Michael Korda (1933-)

When you reach the end of your rope, tie a knot in it and hang on.
Franklin D. Roosevelt (1882-1945)

Perseverance is failing 19 times and succeeding the 20th.
Julie Andrews (1935-)

It is very important to know who you are. To make decisions. To show who you are.
Malala Yousafzai (1997-)

You just can't beat the person who never gives up.
Babe Ruth (1895-1948)

It's always too early to quit.
Norman Vincent Peale (1898-1993)

You need to overcome the tug of people against you as you reach for high goals.
George S. Patton (1885-1945)

Always desire to learn something useful.
Sophocles (497 BC-406 BC)

Pursue one great decisive aim with force and determination.
Carl von Clausewitz (1780-1831)

Do not wait to strike till the iron is hot; but make it hot by striking.
William Butler Yeats (1865-1939)

The will to succeed is important, but what's more important is the will to prepare.

THE GREATEST QUOTES FROM THE GREATEST PEOPLE

Bobby Knight (1940-)

Go for it now. The future is promised to no one.
Wayne Dyer (1940-2015)

You can't build a reputation on what you are going to do.
Henry Ford (1863-1947)

Either I will find a way, or I will make one.
Philip Sidney (1554-1586)

True happiness involves the full use of one's power and talents.
John W. Gardner (1912-2002)

Poverty was the greatest motivating factor in my life.
Jimmy Dean (1928-2010)

Deserve your dream.
Octavio Paz (1914-1998)

Never complain and never explain.
Benjamin Disraeli (1804-1881)

March on. Do not tarry. To go forward is to move toward perfection. March on and fear not the thorns, or the sharp stones on life's path.
Khalil Gibran (1883-1931)

If you don't design your own life plan, chances are you'll fall into someone else's plan. And guess what they have planned for you? Not much.
Jim Rohn (1930-2009)

I'd rather attempt to do something great and fail than to attempt to do nothing and succeed.
Robert H. Schuller (1926-2015)

I've found that luck is quite predictable. If you want more luck, take more chances. Be more active. Show up more often.
Brian Tracy (1944-)

To be a good loser is to learn how to win.
Carl Sandburg (1878-1967)

GEORGE P.

Get action. Seize the moment. Man was never intended to become an oyster.
Theodore Roosevelt (1858-1919)

4 POLITICS

Just because you do not take an interest in politics doesn't mean politics won't take an interest in you.
Pericles (494 BC-429 BC)

In politics, nothing happens by accident. If it happens, you can bet it was planned that way.
Franklin D. Roosevelt (1882-1945)

In our age there is no such thing as 'keeping out of politics.' All issues are political issues and politics itself is a mass of lies, evasions, folly, hatred and schizophrenia.
George Orwell (1903-1950)

Politics is the art of looking for trouble, finding it everywhere, diagnosing it incorrectly and applying the wrong remedies.
Groucho Marx (1890-1977)

The first lesson of economics is scarcity: there is never enough of anything to fully satisfy all those who want it. The first lesson of politics is to disregard the first lesson of economics.
Thomas Sowell (1930-1980)

Politics have no relation to morals.
Niccolo Machiavelli (1469-1527)

The ballot is stronger than the bullet.
Abraham Lincoln (1809-1865)

I must study politics and war that my sons may have liberty to study mathematics and philosophy.
John Adams (1735-1826)

Art, freedom and creativity will change society faster than politics.
Victor Pinchuk (1960-)

One of the key problems today is that politics is such a disgrace, good people don't go into government.
Donald Trump (1946-)

Let us not seek the Republican answer or the Democratic answer, but the right answer. Let us not seek to fix the blame for the past. Let us accept our own responsibility for the future.
John F. Kennedy (1917-1963)

There are many men of principle in both parties in America, but there is no party of principle.
Alexis de Tocqueville (1805-1859)

Suppose you were an idiot and suppose you were a member of Congress; but I repeat myself.
Mark Twain (1835-1910)

One of the penalties for refusing to participate in politics is that you end up being governed by your inferiors.
Plato (427 BC-347 BC)

Those who say religion has nothing to do with politics do not know what religion is.
Mahatma Gandhi (1869-1948)

In politics stupidity is not a handicap.
Napoleon Bonaparte (1769-1821)

I never considered a difference of opinion in politics, in religion, in philosophy, as cause for withdrawing from a friend.
Thomas Jefferson (1743-1826)

If you put the federal government in charge of the Sahara Desert, in 5 years there'd be a shortage of sand.
Milton Friedman (1912-2006)

One of the reasons people hate politics is that truth is rarely a politician's objective. Election and power are.
Cal Thomas (1942-)

The darkest places in hell are reserved for those who maintain their neutrality in times of moral crisis.
Dante Alighieri (1265-1321)

People say satire is dead. It's not dead; it's alive and living in the White House.

THE GREATEST QUOTES FROM THE GREATEST PEOPLE

Robin Williams (1951-2014)

We hang the petty thieves and appoint the great ones to public office.
Aesop (600 BC-564 BC)

The whole aim of practical politics is to keep the populace alarmed (and hence clamorous to be led to safety) by menacing it with an endless series of hobgoblins, all of them imaginary.
H. L. Mencken (1880-1956)

If we don't believe in freedom of expression for people we despise, we don't believe in it at all.
Noam Chomsky (1928-)

When we are sick, we want an uncommon doctor; when we have a construction job to do, we want an uncommon engineer and when we are at war, we want an uncommon general. It is only when we get into politics that we are satisfied with the common man.
Herbert Hoover (1874-1964)

The modern conservative is engaged in one of man's oldest exercises in moral philosophy; that is, the search for a superior moral justification for selfishness.
John Kenneth Galbraith (1908-2006)

There can only be democracy when money is not allowed to be spent in Politics.
Imran Khan (1952-)

Politics is war without bloodshed while war is politics with bloodshed.
Mao Zedong (1893-1976)

No science is immune to the infection of politics and the corruption of power.
Jacob Bronowski (1908-1974)

Community organizing is all about building grassroots support. It's about identifying the people around you with whom you can create a common, passionate cause. And it's about ignoring the conventional wisdom of company politics and instead playing the game by very different rules.
Tom Peters (1942-)

If you have always believed that everyone should play by the same rules and be judged by the same standards, that would have gotten you labeled a radical 60 years ago, a liberal 30 years ago and a racist today.
Thomas Sowell (1930-1980)

In the end, that's what this election is about. Do we participate in a politics of cynicism or a politics of hope?
Barack Obama (1961-)

Establishing lasting peace is the work of education; all politics can do is keep us out of war.
Maria Montessori (1870-1952)

Politics is almost as exciting as war and quite as dangerous. In war you can only be killed once, but in politics many times.
Winston Churchill (1874-1965)

The most practical kind of politics is the politics of decency.
Theodore Roosevelt (1858-1919)

Democracy is when the indigent and not the men of property, are the rulers.
Aristotle (384 BC-322 BC)

We would all like to vote for the best man, but he is never a candidate.
Kin Hubbard (1868-1930)

Voters don't decide issues, they decide who will decide issues.
George Will (1941-)

You want a friend in Washington? Get a dog.
Harry S Truman (1884-1972)

Ninety percent of the politicians give the other ten percent a bad reputation.
Henry Kissinger (1923-)

If you have ten thousand regulations you destroy all respect for the law.
Winston Churchill (1874-1965)

If there is any fixed star in our constitutional constellation, it is that no official, high or petty, can prescribe what shall be orthodox in politics,

nationalism, religion, or other matters of opinion, or force citizens to confess by word or act.
Robert Jackson (1892-1954)

It is enough that the people know there was an election. The people who cast the votes decide nothing. The people who count the votes decide everything.
Joseph Stalin (1878-1953)

In a time of domestic crisis, men of goodwill and generosity should be able to unite regardless of party or politics.
John F. Kennedy (1917-1963)

In this world of sin and sorrow there is always something to be thankful for; as for me, I rejoice that I am not a Republican.
H. L. Mencken (1880-1956)

The career of politics grants a feeling of power. The knowledge of influencing men, of participating in power over them and above all, the feeling of holding in one's hands a nerve fiber of historically important events can elevate the professional politician above everyday routine even when he is placed in formally modest positions.
Max Weber (1864-1920)

Liberalism is trust of the people tempered by prudence. Conservatism is distrust of the people tempered by fear.
William E. Gladstone (1809-1898)

Politics is like football; if you see daylight, go through the hole.
John F. Kennedy (1917-1963)

Never believe anything in politics until it has been officially denied.
Otto von Bismarck (1815-1898)

Politics doesn't make strange bedfellows - marriage does.
Groucho Marx (1890-1977)

Hell hath no fury like a bureaucrat scorned.
Milton Friedman (1912-2006)

Religion forbids us from assuming a God-like character. This is especially true in politics and government, where limiting the power of the state,

division of powers and the doctrine of checks and balances are established in order to prevent accumulation of power that might lead to such Godly claims.
Abdolkarim Soroush (1945-)

There are no morals in politics; there is only expedience. A scoundrel may be of use to us just because he is a scoundrel.
Vladimir Lenin (1870-1924)

One of the things being in politics has taught me is that men are not a reasoned or reasonable sex.
Margaret Thatcher (1925-2013)

That is why everyone in politics and we do it, must make sure that they do not depend on one single interest group. A good compromise is one where everybody makes a contribution.
Angela Merkel (1954-)

A leader in the Democratic Party is a boss, in the Republican Party he is a leader.
Harry S Truman (1884-1972)

To err is human. To blame someone else is politics.
Hubert H. Humphrey (1911-1978)

A conservative is a man with two perfectly good legs who, however, has never learned how to walk forward.
Franklin D. Roosevelt (1882-1945)

When times are tough and people are frustrated and angry and hurting and uncertain, the politics of constant conflict may be good, but what is good politics does not necessarily work in the real world. What works in the real world is cooperation.
William J. Clinton (1946-)

I'm not an old, experienced hand at politics. But I am now seasoned enough to have learned that the hardest thing about any political campaign is how to win without proving that you are unworthy of winning.
Adlai E. Stevenson (1900-1965)

If you believe you can make a difference, not just in politics, in public service, in advocacy around all these important issues, then you have to be

prepared to accept that you are not going to get 100 percent approval.
Hillary Clinton (1947-)

Politics is the entertainment branch of industry.
Frank Zappa (1940-1993)

Politics will eventually be replaced by imagery. The politician will be only too happy to abdicate in favor of his image, because the image will be much more powerful than he could ever be.
Marshall McLuhan (1911-1980)

The revolution is a dictatorship of the exploited against the exploiters.
Fidel Castro (1926-2016)

War is the continuation of politics by other means.
Carl von Clausewitz (1780-1831)

It is impossible to practice parliamentary politics without having patience, decency, politeness and courtesy.
Khaleda Zia (1945-)

The successful revolutionary is a statesman, the unsuccessful one a criminal.
Erich Fromm (1900-1980)

In politics you must always keep running with the pack. The moment that you falter and they sense that you are injured, the rest will turn on you like wolves.
R. A. Butler (1902-1982)

Politics is the ability to foretell what is going to happen tomorrow, next week, next month and next year. And to have the ability afterwards to explain why it didn't happen.
Winston Churchill (1874-1965)

Principles have no real force except when one is well-fed.
Mark Twain (1835-1910)

Politics is the art of controlling your environment.
Hunter S. Thompson (1937-2005)

There is no more independence in politics than there is in jail.
Will Rogers (1879-1935)

Pop culture shapes our ideas of what is normal and what our dreams can be and what our roles are. Politics, of course, decides how the power and the money in the country is distributed. Both are equally important and each affects the other.
Gloria Steinem (1934-)

From politics, it was an easy step to silence.
Jane Austen (1775-1817)

These things will destroy the human race: politics without principle, progress without compassion, wealth without work, learning without silence, religion without fearlessness and worship without awareness.
Anthony de Mello (1931-1987)

Politics is a strong and slow boring of hard boards.
Max Weber (1864-1920)

We have, I fear, confused power with greatness.
Stewart Udall (1920-2010)

Morality binds people into groups. It gives us tribalism, it gives us genocide, war and politics. But it also gives us heroism, altruism and sainthood.
Jonathan Haidt (1963-)

Inflation is as violent as a mugger, as frightening as an armed robber and as deadly as a hit man.
Ronald Reagan (1911-2004)

Like Indiana Jones, I don't like snakes - though that might lead some to ask why I'm in politics.
Theresa May (1956-)

Objective journalism is one of the main reasons that American politics has been allowed to be so corrupt for so long.
Hunter S. Thompson (1937-2005)

5 SUCCESS

By failing to prepare, you are preparing to fail.
Benjamin Franklin (1706-1790)

Success is no accident. It is hard work, perseverance, learning, studying, sacrifice and most of all, love of what you are doing or learning to do.
Pele (1940-)

Put your heart, mind and soul into even your smallest acts. This is the secret of success.
Swami Sivananda (1887-1963)

Your positive action combined with positive thinking results in success.
Shiv Khera (1961-)

Try not to become a man of success, but rather try to become a man of value.
Albert Einstein (1879-1955)

Success is not final, failure is not fatal: it is the courage to continue that counts.
Winston Churchill (1874-1965)

Coming together is a beginning; keeping together is progress; working together is success.
Henry Ford (1863-1947)

Some people dream of success, while other people get up every morning and make it happen.
Wayne Huizenga (1937-)

There are no secrets to success. It is the result of preparation, hard work and learning from failure.
Colin Powell (1937-)

Always be yourself, express yourself, have faith in yourself, do not go out and look for a successful personality and duplicate it.
Bruce Lee (1940-1973)

A strong, positive self-image is the best possible preparation for success.

Joyce Brothers (1927-2013)

Success is a journey, not a destination. The doing is often more important than the outcome.
Arthur Ashe (1943-1993)

I've missed more than 9000 shots in my career. I've lost almost 300 games. 26 times, I've been trusted to take the game winning shot and missed. I've failed over and over and over again in my life. And that is why I succeed.
Michael Jordan (1963-)

For success, attitude is equally as important as ability.
Walter Scott (1771-1832)

Character cannot be developed in ease and quiet. Only through experience of trial and suffering can the soul be strengthened, ambition inspired and success achieved.
Helen Keller (1880-1968)

Success is where preparation and opportunity meet.
Bobby Unser (1934-)

Success is the result of perfection, hard work, learning from failure, loyalty and persistence.
Colin Powell (1937-)

Without continual growth and progress, such words as improvement, achievement and success have no meaning.
Benjamin Franklin (1706-1790)

All you need in this life is ignorance and confidence and then success is sure.
Mark Twain (1835-1910)

The supreme quality for leadership is unquestionably integrity. Without it, no real success is possible, no matter whether it is on a section gang, a football field, in an army, or in an office.
Dwight D. Eisenhower (1890-1969)

Education is the key to success in life and teachers make a lasting impact in the lives of their students.
Solomon Ortiz (1937-)

Success consists of going from failure to failure without loss of enthusiasm.
Winston Churchill (1874-1965)

Patience, persistence and perspiration make an unbeatable combination for success.
Napoleon Hill (1883-1970)

Success is not the key to happiness. Happiness is the key to success. If you love what you are doing, you will be successful.
Albert Schweitzer (1875-1965)

Success is a lousy teacher. It seduces smart people into thinking they can't lose.
Bill Gates (1955-)

Man needs his difficulties because they are necessary to enjoy success.
A. P. J. Abdul Kalam (1931-2015)

Think little goals and expect little achievements. Think big goals and win big success.
David Joseph Schwartz (1927-1987)

Ambition is the path to success. Persistence is the vehicle you arrive in.
Bill Bradley (1943-)

Success does not consist in never making mistakes but in never making the same one a second time.
George Bernard Shaw (1856-1950)

Desire is the key to motivation, but it's determination and commitment to an unrelenting pursuit of your goal - a commitment to excellence - that will enable you to attain the success you seek.
Mario Andretti (1940-)

Success is a science; if you have the conditions, you get the result.
Oscar Wilde (1854-1900)

If everyone is moving forward together, then success takes care of itself.
Henry Ford (1863-1947)

The secret of your success is determined by your daily agenda.

John C. Maxwell (1947-)

Communication - the human connection - is the key to personal and career success.

Paul J. Meyer (1928-2009)

Money won't create success, the freedom to make it will.

Nelson Mandela (1918-2013)

Try to look at your weakness and convert it into your strength. That's success.

Zig Ziglar (1926-2012)

Survival was my only hope, success my only revenge.

Patricia Cornwell (1956-)

The way a team plays as a whole determines its success. You may have the greatest bunch of individual stars in the world, but if they don't play together, the club won't be worth a dime.

Babe Ruth (1895-1948)

Focused, hard work is the real key to success. Keep your eyes on the goal and just keep taking the next step towards completing it. If you aren't sure which way to do something, do it both ways and see which works better.

John Carmack (1970-)

We learned about honesty and integrity - that the truth matters... that you don't take shortcuts or play by your own set of rules... and success doesn't count unless you earn it fair and square.

Michelle Obama (1964-)

The foundation stones for a balanced success are honesty, character, integrity, faith, love and loyalty.

Zig Ziglar (1926-2012)

Take up one idea. Make that one idea your life - think of it, dream of it, live on that idea. Let the brain, muscles, nerves, every part of your body, be full of that idea and just leave every other idea alone. This is the way to success.

Swami Vivekananda (1863-1902)

It's fine to celebrate success but it is more important to heed the lessons of failure.

THE GREATEST QUOTES FROM THE GREATEST PEOPLE

Bill Gates (1955-)

I know of no single formula for success. But over the years I have observed that some attributes of leadership are universal and are often about finding ways of encouraging people to combine their efforts, their talents, their insights, their enthusiasm and their inspiration to work together.

Queen Elizabeth II (1926-)

The road to success is not easy to navigate, but with hard work, drive and passion, it's possible to achieve the American dream.

Tommy Hilfiger (1951-)

The road to success is always under construction.

Arnold Palmer (1929-2016)

The starting point of all achievement is desire.

Napoleon Hill (1883-1970)

Always bear in mind that your own resolution to succeed is more important than any other.

Abraham Lincoln (1809-1865)

Just remember, you can't climb the ladder of success with your hands in your pockets.

Arnold Schwarzenegger (1947-)

Humility is the true key to success. Successful people lose their way at times. They often embrace and overindulge from the fruits of success. Humility halts this arrogance and self-indulging trap. Humble people share the credit and wealth, remaining focused and hungry to continue the journey of success.

Rick Pitino (1952-)

Success makes so many people hate you. I wish it wasn't that way. It would be wonderful to enjoy success without seeing envy in the eyes of those around you.

Marilyn Monroe (1926-1962)

True leaders don't invest in buildings. Jesus never built a building. They invest in people. Why? Because success without a successor is failure. So your legacy should not be in buildings, programs, or projects; your legacy must be in people.

Myles Munroe (1954-2014)

The battle of life is, in most cases, fought uphill; and to win it without a struggle were perhaps to win it without honor. If there were no difficulties there would be no success; if there were nothing to struggle for, there would be nothing to be achieved.
Samuel Smiles (1812-1904)

Don't aim for success if you want it; just do what you love and believe in and it will come naturally.
David Frost (1939-2013)

There is simply no substitute for hard work when it comes to achieving success.
Heather Bresch (1969-)

Success in management requires learning as fast as the world is changing.
Warren Bennis (1925-2014)

You were designed for accomplishment, engineered for success and endowed with the seeds of greatness.
Zig Ziglar (1926-2012)

A little more persistence, a little more effort and what seemed hopeless failure may turn to glorious success.
Elbert Hubbard (1856-1915)

Learning and innovation go hand in hand. The arrogance of success is to think that what you did yesterday will be sufficient for tomorrow.
William Pollard (1828-1893)

Failures, repeated failures, are finger posts on the road to achievement. One fails forward toward success.
C. S. Lewis (1898-1963)

Success is almost totally dependent upon drive and persistence. The extra energy required to make another effort or try another approach is the secret of winning.
Denis Waitley (1933-)

The secret to success is good leadership and good leadership is all about making the lives of your team members or workers better.

Tony Dungy (1955-)

The successful man will profit from his mistakes and try again in a different way.
Dale Carnegie (1888-1955)

Think twice before you speak, because your words and influence will plant the seed of either success or failure in the mind of another.
Napoleon Hill (1883-1970)

If you want to succeed you should strike out on new paths, rather than travel the worn paths of accepted success.
John D. Rockefeller (1839-1937)

The key to success is action and the essential in action is perseverance.
Sun Yat-sen (1866-1925)

One important key to success is self-confidence. An important key to self-confidence is preparation.
Arthur Ashe (1943-1993)

Failure is the key to success; each mistake teaches us something.
Morihei Ueshiba (1883-1969)

Before anything else, preparation is the key to success.
Alexander Graham Bell (1847-1922)

6 UNIQUE SELECTION OF QUOTES

Strive not to be a success, but rather to be of value.
Albert Einstein (1879-1955)

Two roads diverged in a wood and I took the one less traveled by and that has made all the difference.
Robert Frost (1874-1963)

You miss 100% of the shots you don't take.
Wayne Gretzky (1961-)

The most difficult thing is the decision to act, the rest is merely tenacity.
Amelia Earhart (1897-1939)

We become what we think about.
Earl Nightingale (1921-1989)

The most common way people give up their power is by thinking they don't have any.
Alice Walker (1944-)

The mind is everything. What you think you become.
Buddha (563 BC-483 BC)

The best time to plant a tree was 20 years ago. The second-best time is now.
Chinese Proverb

An unexamined life is not worth living.
Socrates (470 BC-399 BC)

Eighty percent of success is showing up.
Woody Allen (1935-)

Do not consider painful what is good for you.
Euripides (480 BC-406 BC)

There are two sides to every question.
Protagoras (485 BC-421 BC)

A multitude of words is no proof of a prudent mind.

THE GREATEST QUOTES FROM THE GREATEST PEOPLE

Thales (624 AD-546 AD)

You can never cross the ocean until you have the courage to lose sight of the shore.
Christopher Columbus (1451-1506)

Waste not fresh tears over old griefs.
Euripides (480 BC-406 BC)

Justice is simply the advantage of the stronger.
Thrasymachus (459 BC-400 BC)

Winning isn't everything but wanting to win is.
Vince Lombardi (1913-1970)

I am not a product of my circumstances. I am a product of my decisions.
Stephen Covey (1932-2012)

Talk sense to a fool and he calls you foolish.
Euripides (480 BC-406 BC)

Every child is an artist. The problem is how to remain an artist once he grows up.
Pablo Picasso (1881-1973)

Those who know how to win are much more numerous than those who know how to make proper use of their victories.
Polybius (205 BC-118 BC)

I've learned that people will forget what you said, people will forget what you did, but people will never forget how you made them feel.
Maya Angelou (1928-2014)

It is frequently a misfortune to have very brilliant men in charge of affairs. They expect too much of ordinary men.
Thucydides (460 BC-395 BC)

The two most important days in your life are the day you are born and the day you find out why.
Mark Twain (1835-1910)

Whatever you can do, or dream you can, begin it. Boldness has genius,

GEORGE P.

power and magic in it.
Johann Wolfgang von Goethe (1749-1832)

The best revenge is massive success.
Frank Sinatra (1915-1998)

Small opportunities are often the beginning of great enterprises.
Demosthenes (384 BC-322 BC)

A man's character is his fate.
Heraclitus (535 BC-475 BC)

The secret of happiness is freedom. The secret of freedom is courage.
Thucydides (460 BC-395 BC)

Life shrinks or expands in proportion to one's courage.
Anais Nin (1903-1977)

The only person you are destined to become is the person you decide to be.
Ralph Waldo Emerson (1803-1882)

There is only one way to avoid criticism: do nothing, say nothing and be nothing.
Aristotle (384 BC-322 BC)

Everything you've ever wanted is on the other side of fear.
George Addair (1823-1899)

If you hear a voice within you say "you cannot paint," then by all means paint and that voice will be silenced.
Vincent Van Gogh (1853-1890)

Though bitter, good medicine cures illness. Though it may hurt, loyal criticism will have beneficial effects.
Sima Qian (145 BC-86 BC)

People often say that motivation doesn't last. Well, neither does bathing, that's why we recommend it daily.
Zig Ziglar (1926-2012)

Ask and it will be given to you; search and you will find; knock and the door will be opened for you.

THE GREATEST QUOTES FROM THE GREATEST PEOPLE

Jesus (0-33)

We can easily forgive a child who is afraid of the dark; the real tragedy of life is when men are afraid of the light.
Plato (427 BC-347 BC)

Certain things catch your eye but pursue only those that capture the heart.
Ancient Indian Proverb

Wait for that wisest of all counselors, Time.
Pericles (494 BC-429 BC)

Believe you can and you're halfway there.
Theodore Roosevelt (1858-1919)

Everything has beauty, but not everyone can see.
Confucius (551 BC-479 BC)

Happiness is not something readymade. It comes from your own actions.
Dalai Lama (1935-)

If you're offered a seat on a rocket ship, don't ask what seat! Just get on.
Sheryl Sandberg (1969-)

Happiness resides not in possessions, and not in gold, happiness dwells in the soul.
Democritus (460 BC-370 BC)

If the wind will not serve, take to the oars.
Latin Proverb

Trees, though they are cut and lopped, grow up again quickly, but if men are destroyed, it is not easy to get them again.
Pericles (494 BC-429 BC)

Knowledge has three degrees opinion, science, illumination. The means or instrument of the first is sense; of the second, dialectic; of the third, intuition.
Plotinus (204 BC-270 BC)

How wonderful it is that nobody needs wait a single moment before starting to improve the world.

GEORGE P.

Anne Frank (1929-1945)

Too many of us are not living our dreams because we are living our fears.
Les Brown (1945-)

Life is not measured by the number of breaths we take, but by the moments that take our breath away.
Maya Angelou (1928-2014)

You can't fall if you don't climb. But there's no joy in living your whole life on the ground.
Unknown

If you want to lift yourself up, lift up someone else.
Booker T. Washington (1856-1915)

I have been impressed with the urgency of doing. Knowing is not enough; we must apply. Being willing is not enough; we must do.
Leonardo da Vinci (1452-1519)

A person who never made a mistake never tried anything new.
Albert Einstein (1879-1955)

The person who says it cannot be done should not interrupt the person who is doing it.
Chinese Proverb

First, have a definite, clear practical ideal; a goal, an objective. Second, have the necessary means to achieve your ends; wisdom, money, materials and methods. Third, adjust all your means to that end.
Aristotle (384 BC-322 BC)

I would rather die of passion than of boredom.
Vincent Van Gogh (1853-1890)

A truly rich man is one whose children run into his arms when his hands are empty.
Unknown

Build your own dreams, or someone else will hire you to build theirs.
Farrah Gray (1984-)

THE GREATEST QUOTES FROM THE GREATEST PEOPLE

Education costs money. But then so does ignorance.
Sir Claus Moser (1922-2015)

It does not matter how slowly you go as long as you do not stop.
Confucius (551 BC-479 BC)

Remember that not getting what you want is sometimes a wonderful stroke of luck.
Dalai Lama (1935-)

There is nothing permanent except change.
Heraclitus (535 BC-475 BC)

It is better to be feared than loved, if you cannot be both.
Niccolo Machiavelli (1469-1527)

Learning never exhausts the mind.
Leonardo da Vinci (1452-1519)

No act of kindness, no matter how small, is ever wasted.
Aesop (600 BC-564 BC)

We know what we are but know not what we may be.
William Shakespeare (1564-1616)

Friends show their love in times of trouble, not in happiness.
Euripides (480 BC-406 BC)

The only true wisdom is in knowing you know nothing.
Socrates (470 BC-399 BC)

In critical moments even the very powerful have need of the weakest.
Aesop (600 BC-564 BC)

Poverty is the parent of revolution and crime.
Aristotle (384 BC-322 BC)

Advice is judged by results, not by intentions.
Cicero (106 BC-43 BC)

Everything has its beauty but not everyone sees it.
Confucius (551 BC-479 BC)

Happiness resides not in possessions and not in gold, happiness dwells in the soul.
Democritus (460 BC-370 BC)

It is not what you do for your children, but what you have taught them to do for themselves, that will make them successful human beings.
Ann Landers (1918-2002)

We must believe that we are gifted for something and that this thing, at whatever cost, must be attained.
Marie Curie (1867-1934)

Wise men speak because they have something to say; Fools because they have to say something.
Plato (427 BC-347 BC)

It is during our darkest moments that we must focus to see the light.
Aristotle (384 BC-322 BC)

7 AUTHORS' BIOGRAPHIES

A. P. J. Abdul Kalam (1931-2015) was the 11th President of India from 2002 to 2007.
Abdolkarim Soroush (1945-) is an Iranian thinker, reformer, Rumi scholar and a former professor of philosophy at the University of Tehran and Imam Khomeini International University.
Abraham Lincoln (1809-1865) was an American politician and lawyer who served as the 16th President of the United States from March 1861 until his assassination in April 1865.
Adlai E. Stevenson (1900-1965) was an American lawyer, politician and diplomat, noted for his intellectual demeanor, eloquent public speaking and promotion of progressive causes in the Democratic Party.
Aesop (600 BC-564 BC) was a Greek fabulist and storyteller credited with several fables now collectively known as Aesop's Fables.
Alain Wertheimer (1948-) is a French businessman based in France who, with his brother Gerard, owns the controlling interest in the House of Chanel and also have an investment in Bell & Ross.
Albert Einstein (1879-1955) was a German-born theoretical physicist. Einstein developed the theory of relativity, one of the two pillars of modern physics. Einstein's work is also known for its influence on the philosophy of science.
Aldous Huxley (1894-1963) was an English writer, novelist, philosopher and prominent member of the Huxley family. He graduated from Balliol College at the University of Oxford with first-class honours in English literature.
Alexis de Tocqueville (1805-1859) was a French diplomat, political scientist and historian. He was best known for his works Democracy in America and The Old Regime and the Revolution.
Alfred A. Montapert (1906-1997) was an author.
Alice Walker (1944-) is an American novelist, short story writer, poet and activist. She wrote the critically acclaimed novel The Color Purple for which she won the National Book Award and the Pulitzer Prize for Fiction.
Allen Ginsberg (1926-1997) was an American poet and one of the leading figures of both the Beat Generation during the 1950s and the counterculture that soon followed.
Amelia Earhart (1897-1939) was an American aviation pioneer and author. Earhart was the first female aviator to fly solo across the Atlantic Ocean. She received the U.S. Distinguished Flying Cross for this accomplishment.
Anais Nin (1903-1977) was an essayist and memoirist born to Cuban parents in France, where she was also raised. She spent some time in Spain and Cuba but lived most of her life in the United States, where she became

an established author.

Angela Merkel (1954-) is a German politician and Chancellor of Germany since 2005. She has also been the leader of the Christian Democratic Union since 10 April 2000.

Ann Landers (1918-2002) was an American advice columnist and eventually a nationwide media celebrity.

Anne Frank (1929-1945) was a German-born diarist. One of the most discussed Jewish victims of the Holocaust, she gained fame posthumously following the publication of The Diary of a Young Girl, in which she documents her life in hiding from 1942 to 1944, during the German occupation of the Netherlands in World War II.

Anthony de Mello (1931-1987) was an Indian Jesuit priest and psychotherapist. A spiritual teacher, writer and public speaker, De Mello wrote several books on spirituality and hosted numerous spiritual retreats and conferences.

Aristotle (384 BC-322 BC) was an ancient Greek philosopher and scientist born in the city of Stagira, Chalkidiki, on the northern periphery of Classical Greece.

Arnold Palmer (1929-2016) was an American professional golfer who is generally regarded as one of the greatest and most charismatic players in the sport's history.

Arnold Schwarzenegger (1947-) is an Austrian-American actor, producer, businessman, investor, author, philanthropist, activist, politician and former professional bodybuilder who holds both Austrian and American citizenship.

Arthur Ashe (1943-1993) was an American professional tennis player. He won three Grand Slam titles.

Audrey Hepburn (1929-1993) was a British actress, model, dancer and humanitarian. Recognized as a film and fashion icon, Hepburn was active during Hollywood's Golden Age.

Ayn Rand (1905-1982) was a Russian-American novelist, philosopher, playwright and screenwriter. She is known for her two best-selling novels, The Fountainhead and Atlas Shrugged and for developing a philosophical system she called Objectivism.

Babe Ruth (1895-1948) was an American professional baseball player whose career in Major League Baseball spanned 22 seasons, from 1914 through 1935.

Barack Obama (1961-) is an American politician who served as the 44th President of the United States from 2009 to 2017. He is the first African American to have served as president.

Benjamin Disraeli (1804-1881) was a British politician and writer who twice served as Prime Minister of the United Kingdom.

Benjamin Franklin (1706-1790) was one of the Founding Fathers of the

United States. Franklin was a renowned polymath and a leading author, printer, political theorist, politician, freemason, postmaster, scientist, inventor, civic activist, statesman and diplomat.

Bertrand Russell (1872-1970) was a British philosopher, logician, mathematician, historian, writer, social critic, political activist and Nobel laureate.

Bill Bradley (1943-) is an American former professional basketball player and politician. He served three terms as a Democratic U.S. Senator from New Jersey.

Bill Gates (1955-) is a co-founder of the Microsoft Corporation and is an American business magnate, investor, author and philanthropist. In 1975, Gates and Paul Allen launched Microsoft, which became the world's largest PC software company. For many years, Gates was rank as the richest person in the world.

Bob Marley (1945-1981) was a Jamaican singer-songwriter, musician and guitarist who achieved international fame and acclaim, blending mostly reggae, ska and rocksteady in his compositions.

Bobby Knight (1940-) is a retired American basketball coach.

Bobby Unser (1934-) is an American former automobile racer.

Booker T. Washington (1856-1915) was an American educator, author, orator and advisor to presidents of the United States. Between 1890 and 1915, Washington was the dominant leader in the African American community.

Bradley Whitford (1959-) is an American actor and political activist.

Brian Tracy (1944-) is a Canadian-born American motivational public speaker and self-development author. He is the author of over seventy books that have been translated into dozens of languages.

Bruce Lee (1940-1973) was a Hong Kong-American actor, film director, martial artist, martial arts instructor, philosopher and founder of the martial art Jeet Kune Do.

Buddha (563 BC-483 BC) was an ascetic and sage, on whose teaching Buddhism was founded.

C. S. Lewis (1898-1963) was a British novelist, poet, academic, medievalist, literary critic, essayist, lay theologian, broadcaster, lecturer and Christian apologist. He held academic positions at both Oxford University and Cambridge University.

Cal Thomas (1942-) is an American syndicated columnist, pundit, author and radio commentator.

Carl Sandburg (1878-1967) was an American poet, writer and editor who won three Pulitzer Prizes: two for his poetry and one for his biography of Abraham Lincoln.

Carl von Clausewitz **(1780-1831)** was a Prussian general and military theorist who stressed the "moral" and political aspects of war. His most notable work, Vom Kriege, was unfinished at his death.

Carlos Slim (1940-) is a Mexican business magnate, investor and philanthropist. From 2010 to 2013, Slim was ranked as the richest person in the world.

Carol Burnett (1933-) is an American actress, comedienne, singer and writer, whose career spans six decades of television.

Cesare Pavese (1908-1950) was an Italian poet, novelist, literary critic and translator. He is widely considered among the major authors of the 20th century in his home country.

Charles R. Swindoll (1934-) is an evangelical Christian pastor, author, educator and radio preacher.

Charlotte Whitton (1896-1975) was a Canadian feminist and mayor of Ottawa. She was the first woman mayor of a major city in Canada, serving from 1951 to 1956 and again from 1960 to 1964.

Christopher Columbus (1451-1506) was an Italian explorer, navigator and colonizer. Born in the Republic of Genoa, under the auspices of the Catholic Monarchs of Spain he completed four voyages across the Atlantic Ocean.

Cicero (106 BC-43 BC) was a Roman politician and lawyer, who served as consul in the year 63 BC. He came from a wealthy municipal family of the Roman equestrian order and is considered one of Rome's greatest orators and prose stylists.

Colin Powell (1937-) is an American statesman and a retired four-star general in the United States Army. Powell was born in Harlem as the son of Jamaican immigrants.

Confucius (551 BC-479 BC) was a Chinese teacher, editor, politician and philosopher of the Spring and Autumn period of Chinese history.

D. H. Lawrence (1885-1930) was an English novelist, poet, playwright, essayist, literary critic and painter.

Dalai Lama (1935-) is the current Dalai Lama. Dalai Lamas are important monks of the Gelug school, the newest school of Tibetan Buddhism which is nominally headed by the Ganden Tripas.

Dale Carnegie (1888-1955) was an American writer and lecturer and the developer of famous courses in self-improvement, salesmanship, corporate training, public speaking and interpersonal skills.

Dan Millman (1946-) is an American author and lecturer in the personal development field.

Dante Alighieri (1265-1321) was a major Italian poet of the Late Middle Ages.

Dave Ramsey (1960-) is an American businessman, author, radio host, television personality and motivational speaker.

David Frost (1939-2013) was an English journalist, comedian, writer, media personality and television host.

David Joseph Schwartz (1927-1987) was an American motivational writer and a professor at Georgia State University.

Democritus (460 BC-370 BC) was an influential Ancient Greek pre-Socratic philosopher primarily remembered today for his formulation of an atomic theory of the universe.

Demosthenes (384 BC-322 BC) was a Greek statesman and orator of ancient Athens. His orations constitute a significant expression of contemporary Athenian intellectual prowess and provide an insight into the politics and culture of ancient Greece during the 4th century BC.

Denis Diderot (1713-1784) was a French philosopher, art critic and writer. He was a prominent figure during the Enlightenment and is best known for serving as co-founder, chief editor and contributor to the Encyclopedia along with Jean le Rond d'Alembert.

Denis Waitley (1933-) is an American motivational speaker, writer and consultant.

Don Marquis (1878-1937) was a humorist, journalist and author. He was variously a novelist, poet, newspaper columnist and playwright. He is remembered best for creating the characters Archy and Mehitabel, supposed authors of humorous verse.

Donald Trump (1946-) is the 45th President of the United States. Before entering politics, he was a businessman and television personality.

Drew Houston (1983-) is an American Internet entrepreneur who is best known for being the founder and CEO of Dropbox, an online backup and storage service.

Dwight D. Eisenhower (1890-1969) was an American politician and Army general who served as the 34th President of the United States from 1953 until 1961.

Earl Nightingale (1921-1989) was an American radio speaker and author, dealing mostly with the subjects of human character development, motivation, excellence and meaningful existence.

Eddie Cantor (1892-1964) was an American "illustrated song" performer, comedian, dancer, singer, actor and songwriter.

Edward Gibbon (1737-1794) was an English historian, writer and Member of Parliament. His most important work is The History of the Decline and Fall of the Roman Empire.

Elbert Hubbard (1856-1915) was an American writer, publisher, artist and philosopher.

Eleanor Roosevelt (1884-1962) was an American politician, diplomat and activist. She was the longest-serving First Lady of the United States.

Elon Musk (1971-) is a South African-born Canadian American business magnate, investor, engineer and inventor.

Epictetus (55-135) was a Greek Stoic philosopher.

Erich Fromm (1900-1980) was a German social psychologist, psychoanalyst, sociologist, humanistic philosopher and democratic socialist.
Euripides (480 BC-406 BC) was a tragedian of classical Athens. Along with Aeschylus and Sophocles, he is one of the three ancient Greek tragedians several whose plays have survived.
Farrah Gray (1984-) is an American businessman, investor, author, columnist and motivational speaker.
Fidel Castro (1926-2016) was a Cuban revolutionary and politician who governed the Republic of Cuba as Prime Minister from 1959 to 1976 and then as President from 1976 to 2008.
Florence Nightingale (1820-1910) was an English social reformer and statistician and the founder of modern nursing.
Frank Sinatra (1915-1998) was an American singer, actor and producer who was one of the most popular and influential musical artists of the 20th century.
Frank Zappa (1940-1993) was an American musician, activist and filmmaker.
Franklin D. Roosevelt (1882-1945) was an American statesman and political leader who served as the 32nd President of the United States from 1933 until his death in 1945.
Fred Wilson (1961-) is an American businessman, venture capitalist and blogger.
Friedrich Nietzsche (1844-1900) was a German philosopher, cultural critic, poet, philologist and Latin and Greek scholar whose work has exerted a profound influence on Western philosophy and modern intellectual history.
George Addair (1823-1899) was a real-estate developer in post Civil War Atlanta.
George Bernard Shaw (1856-1950) was an Irish playwright, critic and polemicist whose influence on Western theatre, culture and politics extended from the 1880s to his death and beyond.
George Herbert (1593-1633) was a Welsh-born poet, orator and Anglican priest. Herbert's poetry is associated with the writings of the metaphysical poets and he is recognized as "one of the foremost British devotional lyricists.
George Orwell (1903-1950) was an English novelist, essayist, journalist and critic.
George S. Patton (1885-1945) was a senior officer of the United States Army who commanded the U.S. Seventh Army in the Mediterranean and European theaters of World War II but is best known for his leadership of the U.S.
George Sand (1804-1876) was a French novelist and memoirist.
George Will (1941-) is a Pulitzer Prize-winning conservative political

commentator.

Gloria Steinem (1934-) is an American feminist, journalist and social and political activist, who became nationally recognized as a leader and a spokeswoman for the American feminist movement in the late 1960s and early 1970s.

Gordon B. Hinckley (1910-2008) was an American religious leader and author who served as the 15th President of The Church of Jesus Christ of Latter-day Saints from March 12, 1995, until his death.

Greg Brenneman (1961-) is an American businessman.

Groucho Marx (1890-1977) was an American writer, comedian, stage, film and television star.

H. G. Wells (1866-1946) was an English writer. He was prolific in many genres, including the novel, history, politics, social commentary and textbooks and rules for war games.

H. L. Mencken (1880-1956) was an American journalist, satirist, cultural critic and scholar of American English.

Harriet Beecher Stowe (1811-1896) was an American abolitionist and author.

Harry S Truman (1884-1972) was the 33rd President of the United States, assuming that office upon the death of Franklin D. Roosevelt during the waning months of World War II.

Harvey Mackay (1932-) is a businessman, author and syndicated columnist with Universal Uclick.

Heather Bresch (1969-) is an American business executive.

Helen Keller (1880-1968) was an American author, political activist and lecturer. She was the first deaf-blind person to earn a bachelor of arts degree.

Helen Rowland (1875-1950) was an American journalist and humorist.

Henri Nouwen (1932-1996) was a Dutch Catholic priest, professor, writer and theologian. His interests were rooted primarily in psychology, pastoral ministry, spirituality, social justice and community.

Henry Drummond (1851-1897) was a Scottish evangelist, biologist, writer and lecturer.

Henry Ford (1863-1947) was an American captain of industry and a business magnate, the founder of the Ford Motor Company and the sponsor of the development of the assembly line technique of mass production.

Henry Kissinger (1923-) is an American diplomat and political scientist who served as the United States Secretary of State and National Security Advisor under the presidential administrations of Richard Nixon and Gerald Ford.

Henry Rollins (1961-) is an American musician, actor and writer.

Heraclitus (535 BC-475 BC) was a pre-Socratic Greek philosopher.

Herbert Hoover (1874-1964) was an American politician who served as the 31st President of the United States from 1929 to 1933 during the Great Depression.

Hillary Clinton (1947-) is an American politician who was the 67th United States Secretary of State from 2009 to 2013, U.S. Senator from New York from 2001 to 2009, First Lady of the United States from 1993 to 2001.

Hubert H. Humphrey (1911-1978) was an American politician who served as the 38th Vice President of the United States under President Lyndon B. Johnson from 1965 to 1969.

Hunter S. Thompson (1937-2005) was an American journalist and author and the founder of the gonzo journalism movement.

Imran Khan (1952-) is a Pakistani politician, former cricketer and philanthropist who leads the Pakistan Movement of Justice and serves as a member of the National Assembly.

Jack Canfield (1944-) is an American author, motivational speaker, seminar leader, corporate trainer and entrepreneur.

Jack Welch (1935-) is an American retired business executive, author and chemical engineer.

Jacob Bronowski (1908-1974) was a British mathematician, historian of science, theatre author, poet and inventor.

Jane Austen (1775-1817) was an English novelist known primarily for her six major novels, which interpret, critique and comment upon the British landed gentry at the end of the 18th century.

Jean Paul (1763-1825) is a French haute couture and prêt-à-porter fashion designer.

Jeff Bezos (1964-) is an American technology and retail entrepreneur, investor, computer scientist and philanthropist who is best known as the founder, chairman and chief executive officer of Amazon.com, the world's largest online shopping retailer.

Jesus (0-33) was a Jewish preacher and religious leader who became the central figure of Christianity. Christians believe him to be the Son of God and the awaited Messiah (Christ) prophesied in the Old Testament.

Jim Rohn (1930-2009) was an American entrepreneur, author and motivational speaker.

Jimmy Dean (1928-2010) was an American country music singer, television host, actor and businessman.

Joan of Arc (1412-1431) is considered a heroine of France for her role during the Lancastrian phase of the Hundred Years' War and was canonized as a Roman Catholic saint.

Johann Wolfgang von Goethe (1749-1832) was a German writer and statesman. His works include epic and lyric poetry; prose and verse dramas; memoirs; an autobiography; literary and aesthetic criticism; treatises on botany, anatomy and colour; and four novels.

John Adams (1735-1826) was an American patriot who served as the second President of the United States and the first Vice President.

John Burroughs (1837-1921) was an American naturalist and nature essayist, active in the U.S. conservation movement. The first of his essay collections was Wake-Robin in 1871.

John C. Maxwell (1947-) is an American author, speaker and pastor who has written many books, primarily focusing on leadership.

John Carmack (1970-) is an American game programmer, aerospace and virtual reality engineer.

John D. Rockefeller (1839-1937) was an American oil industry business magnate and philanthropist. Widely considered the wealthiest American of all time and the richest person in modern history.

John Dewey (1859-1952) was an American philosopher, psychologist and educational reformer whose ideas have been influential in education and social reform.

John F. Kennedy (1917-1963) was an American statesman who served as the 35th President of the United States from January 1961 until his assassination in November 1963.

John Kenneth Galbraith (1908-2006) was a Canadian-born economist, public official and diplomat and a leading proponent of 20th-century American liberalism.

John W. Gardner (1912-2002) was Secretary of Health, Education and Welfare under President Lyndon Johnson.

John Wooden (1910-2010) was an American basketball player and head coach at the University of California at Los Angeles.

Jonathan Haidt (1963-) is an American social psychologist and Professor of Ethical Leadership at New York University's Stern School of Business.

Joseph Campbell (1904-1987) was an American mythologist, writer and lecturer.

Joseph Stalin (1878-1953) was a Georgian-born Soviet revolutionary and political leader who governed the Soviet Union as its dictator from the mid-1920s until his death in 1953.

Joyce Brothers (1927-2013) was an American psychologist, television personality and columnist, who wrote a daily newspaper advice column from 1960 to 2013.

Joyce Meyer (1943-) is a Charismatic Christian author and speaker.

Julie Andrews (1935-) is an English actress, singer and author.

Kenneth Branagh (1960-) is a Northern Irish actor, director, producer and screenwriter.

Khaleda Zia (1945-) is a Bangladeshi politician who was the Prime Minister of Bangladesh from 1991 to 1996 and again from 2001 to 2006.

Khalil Gibran (1883-1931) was a Lebanese writer, poet and visual artist.

Kin Hubbard (1868-1930) was an American cartoonist, humorist and journalist.

Lakshmi Mittal (1950-) is an Indian steel magnate, based in the United Kingdom. He is the chairman and CEO of ArcelorMittal, the world's largest steelmaking company.

Lao Tzu (604 BC-531 BC) was an ancient Chinese philosopher and writer. He is known as the reputed author of the Tao Te Ching, the founder of philosophical Taoism and a deity in religious Taoism and traditional Chinese religions.

Leo Burnett (1891-1971) was an American advertising executive.

Leo Buscaglia (1924-1998) was an American author and motivational speaker and a professor in the Department of Special Education at the University of Southern California.

Leonardo da Vinci (1452-1519) was an Italian Renaissance polymath whose areas of interest included invention, painting, sculpting, architecture, science, music, mathematics, engineering, literature, anatomy, geology, astronomy, botany, writing, history and cartography.

Les Brown (1945-) is an American motivational speaker, author, radio DJ, former television host and former politician.

Lindsay Fox (1937-) is an Australian businessman.

Lord Acton (1834-1902) was an English Catholic historian, politician and writer.

Lucius Annaeus Seneca (4 BC-65) was a Roman Stoic philosopher, statesman, dramatist and—in one work—humorist of the Silver Age of Latin literature.

Magdalena Neuner (1987-) is a retired German professional biathlete.

Mahatma Gandhi (1869-1948) was the leader of the Indian independence movement against British rule. Employing nonviolent civil disobedience, Gandhi led India to independence and inspired movements for civil rights and freedom across the world.

Malala Yousafzai (1997-) is a Pakistani activist for female education and the youngest-ever Nobel Prize laureate.

Malcolm Forbes (1919-1990) was an American entrepreneur most prominently known as the publisher of Forbes magazine, founded by his father B. C. Forbes.

Mao Zedong (1893-1976) was a Chinese communist revolutionary, poet, political theorist and founding father of the People's Republic of China, which he governed as the Chairman of the Communist Party of China from its establishment in 1949 until his death in 1976.

Marcus Aurelius (121-180) was Emperor of Rome from 161 to 180. He ruled with Lucius Verus as co-emperor from 161 until Verus' death in 169. Marcus Aurelius was the last of the so-called Five Good Emperors.

Margaret Thatcher (1925-2013) was a British stateswoman who was Prime Minister of the United Kingdom from 1979 to 1990 and Leader of the Conservative Party from 1975 to 1990.

Maria Montessori (1870-1952) was an Italian physician and educator best known for the philosophy of education that bears her name and her writing on scientific pedagogy.

Marie Curie (1867-1934) was a Polish and naturalized-French physicist and chemist who conducted pioneering research on radioactivity. She was the first woman to win a Nobel Prize, the first person and only woman to win twice, the only person to win a Nobel Prize in two different sciences and was part of the Curie family legacy of five Nobel Prizes.

Marilyn Monroe (1926-1962) was an American actress and model. Famous for playing comic "dumb blonde" characters, she became one of the most popular sex symbols of the 1950s and was emblematic of the era's attitudes towards sexuality.

Mario Andretti (1940-) is an Italian-born American former racing driver, one of the most successful Americans in the history of the sport.

Marissa Mayer (1975-) is an American information technology executive, formerly serving as the president and CEO of Yahoo.

Mark Cuban (1958-) is an American businessman, investor, author, television personality and philanthropist. He is the owner of the NBA's Dallas Mavericks.

Mark Twain (1835-1910) was an American writer, humorist, entrepreneur, publisher and lecturer.

Mark Zuckerberg (1984-) is an American computer programmer and Internet entrepreneur. He is a co-founder of Facebook and currently operates as its chairman and chief executive officer.

Marshall McLuhan (1911-1980) was a Canadian professor, philosopher and public intellectual.

Martin Luther King, Jr. (1929-1968) was an American Baptist minister and activist who became the most visible spokesperson and leader in the Civil Rights Movement.

Mary Kay Ash (1918-2001) was an American businesswoman.

Max de Pree (1924-2017) as an American businessman and writer.

Max Weber (1864-1920) was a German sociologist, philosopher, jurist, political economist and the husband of Marianne Schnitger. His ideas profoundly influenced social theory and social research.

Maya Angelou (1928-2014) was an American poet, memoirist and civil rights activist.

Melody Beattie (1948-) is an American author of self-help books on codependent relationships.

Meredith Whitney (1969-) is an American financial analyst.

Michael Eisner (1942-) is an American businessman. Eisner was the Chairman and Chief Executive Officer of The Walt Disney Company from 1984 until 2005.

Michael Jordan (1963-) is an American retired professional basketball player, businessman and principal owner and chairman of the Charlotte Hornets. His biography on the NBA website states: "By acclamation, Michael Jordan is the greatest basketball player of all time".
Michael Korda (1933-) is an English-born writer and novelist.
Michael LeBoeuf (1942-) is an American business author and former management professor at the University of New Orleans.
Michelle Obama (1964-) is an American lawyer and writer who was First Lady of the United States from 2009 to 2017. She is married to the 44th President of the United States, Barack Obama and is the first African-American First Lady.
Milan Kundera (1929-) is a Czech-born French writer.
Milton Friedman (1912-2006) was an American economist who received the 1976 Nobel Memorial Prize in Economic Sciences for his research on consumption analysis, monetary history and theory and the complexity of stabilization policy.
Mohammed bin Rashid Al Maktoum (1949-) is the Vice President and Prime Minister of the United Arab Emirates and ruler of the Emirate of Dubai.
Morgan Freeman (1937-) is an American actor, producer and narrator. Freeman won an Academy Award in 2005, a Golden Globe Award and a Screen Actors Guild Award.
Muhammad Ali (1942-2016) was an American professional boxer and activist. He is widely regarded as one of the most significant and celebrated sports figures of the 20th century.
Muhammad Iqbal (1877-1938) was a Kashmiri descent poet, philosopher and politician, as well as an academic, barrister and scholar in British India who is widely regarded as having inspired the Pakistan Movement.
Myles Munroe (1954-2014) was a Bahamian evangelist and ordained minister avid professor of the Kingdom of God, author, speaker and leadership consultant who founded and led the Bahamas Faith Ministries International and Myles Munroe International.
Napoleon Bonaparte (1769-1821) was a French military and political leader who rose to prominence during the French Revolution and led several successful campaigns during the French Revolutionary Wars.
Napoleon Hill (1883-1970) was an American self-help author. He is well known for his book Think and Grow Rich which is among the top 10 best selling self-help books of all time.
Nelson Mandela (1918-2013) was a South African anti-apartheid revolutionary, politician and philanthropist, who served as President of South Africa from 1994 to 1999.
Niccolo Machiavelli (1469-1527) was an Italian diplomat, politician, historian, philosopher, humanist and writer of the Renaissance period. He

has often been called the father of modern political science. He wrote his most renowned work The Prince (Il Principe) in 1513.

Nikos Kazantzakis (1883-1957) was a Greek writer. Widely considered a giant of modern Greek literature, he was nominated for the Nobel Prize in Literature in nine different years.

Noam Chomsky (1928-) is an American linguist, philosopher, cognitive scientist, historian, social critic and political activist.

Norman Cousins (1915-1990) was an American political journalist, author, professor and world peace advocate.

Norman Vincent Peale (1898-1993) was an American minister and author known for his work in popularizing the concept of positive thinking, especially through his best-selling book The Power of Positive Thinking.

Octavio Paz (1914-1998) was a Mexican poet and diplomat.

Og Mandino (1923-1996) was an American author. His books have sold over 50 million copies and have been translated into over twenty-five different languages.

Oliver Goldsmith (1728-1774) was an Irish novelist, playwright and poet, who is best known for his novel The Vicar of Wakefield, his pastoral poem The Deserted Village and his plays The Good-Natur'd Man and She Stoops to Conquer.

Omar Khayyam (1048-1131) was a Persian mathematician, astronomer, philosopher and poet, widely considered to be one of the most influential thinkers of the Middle Ages. He also wrote treatises on physics and music theory.

Oprah Winfrey (1954-) is an American media proprietor, talk show host, actress, producer and philanthropist.

Orison Swett Marden (1848-1924) was an American inspirational author who wrote about achieving success in life and founded SUCCESS magazine in 1897.

Oscar Wilde (1854-1900) was a prolific Irish writer who wrote plays, fiction, essays and poetry. After writing in different forms throughout the 1880s, he became one of London's most popular playwrights in the early 1890s.

Otto von Bismarck (1815-1898) was a conservative Prussian statesman who dominated German and European affairs from the 1860s until 1890.

Pablo Picasso (1881-1973) was a Spanish painter, sculptor, printmaker, ceramicist, stage designer, poet and playwright who spent most of his adult life in France.

Patricia Cornwell (1956-) is a contemporary American crime writer. Her books have sold more than 100 million copies.

Paul J. Meyer (1928-2009) is considered the pioneer of the self-improvement industry. His 24 full-length programs have sold more than two billion dollars worldwide, more than any other author in this field, living or deceased.

Paulo Coelho (1947-) is a Brazilian lyricist and novelist and the recipient of numerous international awards. He is best known for his widely translated novel The Alchemist.

Pele (1940-) is a retired Brazilian professional footballer who played as a forward. He is widely regarded as the greatest football player of all time.

Pericles (494 BC-429 BC) was a prominent and influential Greek statesman, orator and general of Athens during the Golden Age—specifically the time between the Persian and Peloponnesian wars.

Peter Drucker (1909-2005) was an Austrian-born American management consultant, educator and author, whose writings contributed to the philosophical and practical foundations of the modern business corporation.

Phil Knight (1938-) is an American business magnate and philanthropist.

Philip Green (1952-) is a British businessman.

Philip Sidney (1554-1586) as an English poet, courtier, scholar and soldier, who is remembered as one of the most prominent figures of the Elizabethan age.

Plato (427 BC-347 BC) was a philosopher in Classical Greece and the founder of the Academy in Athens, the first institution of higher learning in the Western world.

Plotinus (204 BC-270 BC) was a major Greek-speaking philosopher of the ancient world. In his philosophy, there are three principles: the One, the Intellect, and the Soul. His teacher was Ammonius Saccas and he is of the Platonic tradition.

Polybius (205 BC-118 BC) was a Greek historian of the Hellenistic period noted for his work, The Histories, which covered the period of 264–146 BC in detail.

Pope John XXIII (1881-1963) reigned as Pope from 28 October 1958 to his death in 1963 and was canonized on 27 April 2014.

Protagoras (485 BC-421 BC) was a pre-Socratic Greek philosopher and is numbered as one of the sophists by Plato. In his dialogue, Protagoras, Plato credits him with having invented the role of the professional sophist.

Queen Elizabeth II (1926-) has been Queen of the United Kingdom, Canada, Australia and New Zealand since 6 February 1952.

R. A. Butler (1902-1982) was a prominent British Conservative politician.

Rabindranath Tagore (1861-1941) was a Bengali polymath who reshaped Bengali literature and music, as well as Indian art with Contextual Modernism in the late 19th and early 20th centuries.

Ralph Marston (1907-1967) was a professional football player.

Ralph Waldo Emerson (1803-1882) was an American essayist, lecturer and poet who led the transcendentalist movement of the mid-19th century.

Richard Branson (1950-) is an English business magnate, investor and philanthropist. He founded the Virgin Group, which controls more than 400 companies.

Rick Pitino (1952-) is an American basketball coach.

Robert Frost (1874-1963) was an American poet. He is highly regarded for his realistic depictions of rural life and his command of American colloquial speech.

Robert H. Schuller (1926-2015) was an American Christian televangelist, pastor, motivational speaker and author.

Robert Jackson (1892-1954) was an American attorney and judge who served as an Associate Justice of the United States Supreme Court.

Robert Kiyosaki (1947-) is an American businessman and author.

Robin S. Sharma (1965-) is a Canadian writer and leadership speaker.

Robin Williams (1951-2014) was an American stand-up comedian and actor.

Ronald Reagan (1911-2004) was an American politician and actor who served as the 40th President of the United States from 1981 to 1989.

Sai Baba (1835-1918) was an Indian spiritual master who is regarded by his devotees as a saint, a fakir, a satguru and an incarnation of Lord Shiva.

Sam Levenson (1911-1980) was an American humorist, writer, teacher, television host and journalist.

Sam Walton (1918-1992) was an American businessman and entrepreneur best known for founding the retailers Walmart and Sam's Club.

Samuel Beckett (1906-1989) was an Irish avant-garde novelist, playwright, theatre director and poet.

Samuel Smiles (1812-1904) was a Scottish author and government reformer.

Sanford I. Weill (1933-) is an American banker, financier and philanthropist. He is a former chief executive and chairman of Citigroup.

Satya Nadella (1967-) is an Indian American business executive. He is the current Chief Executive Officer of Microsoft.

Sheryl Sandberg (1969-) is an American technology executive, activist and author. She is the chief operating officer of Facebook.

Shiv Khera (1961-) is an Indian author of self-help books.

Sholem Aleichem (1859-1916) was a leading Yiddish author and playwright.

Sima Qian (145 BC-86 BC) was a Chinese historian of the Han dynasty. He is considered the father of Chinese historiography for his Records of the Grand Historian, a Jizhuanti-style (history presented in a series of biographies) general history of China, covering more than two thousand years from the Yellow Emperor to his time, during the reign of Emperor Wu of Han, a work that had much influence for centuries afterwards on history-writing not only in China, but in Korea, Japan and Vietnam as well.

Simone de Beauvoir (1908-1986) was a French writer, intellectual,

existentialist philosopher, political activist, feminist and social theorist.
Simone Weil (1909-1943) was a French philosopher, mystic and political activist.
Sir Claus Moser (1922-2015) was a British statistician who made major contributions in both academia and the Civil Service.
Socrates (470 BC-399 BC) was a classical Greek (Athenian) philosopher credited as one of the founders of Western philosophy. He is an enigmatic figure known chiefly through the accounts of classical writers, especially the writings of his students Plato and Xenophon and the plays of his contemporary Aristophanes.
Solomon Ortiz (1937-) is the former U.S. Representative for Texas's 27th congressional district, based in Corpus Christi, serving from 1983 until 2011.
Sophocles (497 BC-406 BC) is one of three ancient Greek tragedians whose plays have survived. His first plays were written later than those of Aeschylus and earlier than or contemporary with those of Euripides.
St. Jerome (347-420) was a priest, confessor, theologian and historian.
Stephen Covey (1932-2012) was an American educator, author, businessman and keynote speaker. His most popular book was The 7 Habits of Highly Effective People.
Stephen Hawking (1942-) is an English theoretical physicist, cosmologist, author and Director of Research at the Centre for Theoretical Cosmology within the University of Cambridge.
Steve Jobs (1955-2011) was an American entrepreneur, businessman, inventor and industrial designer.
Stewart Udall (1920-2010) was an American politician and later, a federal government official.
Swami Sivananda (1887-1963) was a Hindu spiritual teacher and a proponent of Yoga and Vedanta. Sivananda was born Kuppuswami in Pattamadai, in the Tirunelveli district of Tamil Nadu.
Swami Vivekananda (1863-1902) was an Indian Hindu monk, a chief disciple of the 19th-century Indian mystic Ramakrishna.
Tecumseh (1768-1813) was a Native American Shawnee warrior and chief, who became the primary leader of a large, multi-tribal confederacy in the early years of the nineteenth century.
Ted Turner (1938-) is an American media mogul, philanthropist and a businessman,
Thales (624 AD-546 AD) was a pre-Socratic Greek philosopher, mathematician and astronomer from Miletus in Asia Minor (present-day Milet in Turkey). He was one of the Seven Sages of Greece. Many, most notably Aristotle, regarded him as the first philosopher in the Greek tradition, and he is otherwise historically recognized as the first individual in Western civilization known to have entertained and engaged in scientific

philosophy.

Theodore Roosevelt (1858-1919) was an American statesman, author, explorer, soldier, naturalist and reformer who served as the 26th President of the United States from 1901 to 1909.

Theresa May (1956-) is a British politician who has served as Prime Minister of the United Kingdom and Leader of the Conservative Party since 2016, the second woman to hold both positions after Margaret Thatcher.

Thich Nhat Hanh (1926-) is a Vietnamese Buddhist monk and peace activist.

Thomas A. Edison (1847-1931) was an American inventor and businessman, who has been described as America's greatest inventor.

Thomas Chandler Haliburton (1796-1865) was a Nova Scotian politician, judge and author.

Thomas J. Stanley (1944-2015) was an American writer and business theorist.

Thomas Jefferson (1743-1826) was an American Founding Father who was the principal author of the Declaration of Independence and later served as the third President of the United States from 1801 to 1809.

Thomas Paine (1737-1809) was an English-American political activist, philosopher, political theorist and revolutionary.

Thomas Perez (1961-) is an American politician and attorney.

Thomas Sowell (1930-1980) is an American economist, turned social theorist, political philosopher and author.

Thrasymachus (459 BC-400 BC) was a sophist of Ancient Greece best known as a character in Plato's Republic.

Thucydides (460 BC-395 BC) was an Athenian historian and general. His History of the Peloponnesian War recounts the 5th-century BC war between Sparta and Athens until the year 411 BC.

Tilman J. Fertitta (1957-) is an American businessman and television personality.

Tina Turner (1939-) is an American-born Swiss recording singer, songwriter, dancer, actress and author.

Tom Peters (1942-) is an American writer on business management practices, best known for In Search of Excellence.

Tom Stoppard (1937-) is a Czech-born British playwright and screenwriter, knighted in 1997.

Tommy Hilfiger (1951-) is an American fashion designer best known for founding the lifestyle brand Tommy Hilfiger Corporation in 1985.

Tony Dungy (1955-) is a former professional American football player and coach in the National Football League.

Tony Robbins (1960-) is an American author, entrepreneur, philanthropist and life coach.

Victor Kiam (1926-2001) was an American entrepreneur, TV spokesman and the owner of the New England Patriots football team from 1988–1991.

Victor Pinchuk (1960-) is a Ukrainian businessman and philanthropist.

Vince Lombardi (1913-1970) was an American football player, coach and executive in the National Football League.

Vincent Van Gogh (1853-1890) was a Dutch Post-Impressionist painter who is among the most famous and influential figures in the history of Western art.

Vladimir Lenin (1870-1924) was a Russian communist revolutionary, politician and political theorist who served as head of government of the Russian Republic from 1917 to 1918, of the Russian Soviet Federative Socialist Republic from 1918 to 1924 and of the Soviet Union from 1922 to 1924.

Vladimir Putin (1952-) is the current President of Russia, holding the office since 7 May 2012. He was Prime Minister from 1999 to 2000, President from 2000 to 2008 and again Prime Minister from 2008 to 2012.

Voltaire (1694-1778) was a French Enlightenment writer, historian and philosopher famous for his wit, his attacks on the established Catholic Church and his advocacy of freedom of religion, freedom of speech and separation of church and state.

W. Clement Stone (1902-2002) was a businessman, philanthropist and New Thought self-help book author.

Walt Disney (1901-1966) was an American entrepreneur, animator, voice actor and film producer. A pioneer of the American animation industry, he introduced several developments in the production of cartoons.

Walter Anderson (1903-1965) was an American painter, writer and naturalist.

Walter Elliot (1888-1958) was a prominent Scottish Unionist Party politician in the interwar years. His most important role was as Secretary of State for Scotland.

Walter Scott (1771-1832) was a Scottish historical novelist, playwright and poet. Many of his works remain classics of both English-language literature and Scottish literature.

Warren Bennis (1925-2014) was an American scholar, organizational consultant and author, widely regarded as a pioneer of the contemporary field of Leadership studies.

Warren Buffett (1930-) is an American business magnate, investor, philanthropist. Buffett serves as the Chief Executive Officer and Chairman of Berkshire Hathaway. Buffett is one of the richest persons in the world.

Wayne Dyer (1940-2015) was an American philosopher, self-help author and a motivational speaker.

Wayne Gretzky (1961-) is a Canadian former professional ice hockey player and former head coach.

Wayne Huizenga (1937-) is an American businessman and entrepreneur. He has been involved in the founding of three Fortune 500 corporations and is responsible for six New York Stock Exchange listed companies.

Will Rogers (1879-1935) was a stage and motion picture actor, vaudeville performer, American cowboy, humorist, newspaper columnist and social commentator.

William Barclay (1907-1978) was a Scottish author, radio and television presenter, Church of Scotland minister and Professor of Divinity and Biblical Criticism at the University of Glasgow.

William Blake (1757-1827) was an English poet, painter and printmaker. Largely unrecognised during his lifetime, Blake is now considered a seminal figure in the history of the poetry and visual arts of the Romantic Age.

William Butler Yeats (1865-1939) was an Irish poet and one of the foremost figures of 20th-century literature. A pillar of both the Irish and British literary establishments, he helped to find the Abbey Theatre and in his later years served as an Irish Senator for two terms.

William E. Gladstone (1809-1898) was a British Liberal and earlier conservative politician. In a career lasting over 60 years, he served as Prime Minister four separate times, more than any other person and served as Chancellor of the Exchequer four times. Gladstone was also Britain's oldest Prime Minister.

William J. Clinton (1946-) is an American politician who served as the 42nd President of the United States from 1993 to 2001.

William James (1842-1910) was an American philosopher and psychologist who was also trained as a physician. The first educator to offer a psychology course in the United States, James was one of the leading thinkers of the late nineteenth century and is believed by many to be one of the most influential philosophers the United States has ever produced.

William Pollard (1828-1893) was a physicist and an Episcopal priest.

William Shakespeare (1564-1616) was an English poet, playwright and actor, widely regarded as the greatest writer in the English language and the world's pre-eminent dramatist. He is often called England's national poet and the "Bard of Avon".

Winston Churchill (1874-1965) was a British politician and statesman who served as the Prime Minister of the United Kingdom from 1940 to 1945 and again from 1951 to 1955.

Woodrow Wilson (1856-1924) was an American politician and academic who served as the 28th President of the United States from 1913 to 1921.

Woody Allen (1935-) is an American filmmaker, writer, actor, comedian and musician.

Yoko Ono (1933-) is a Japanese multimedia artist, singer, songwriter and peace activist who is also known for her work in performance art and filmmaking.

Zig Ziglar (1926-2012) was an American author, salesman and motivational speaker.

www.ingramcontent.com/pod-product-compliance
Lightning Source LLC
Chambersburg PA
CBHW031542210526
45464CB00003B/1108